BR BLUE No 5

PASSENGER and PARCELS
1975 - 1990

John Dedman

N.B.

© Kevin Robertson (Noodle Books) and John Dedman 2012

ISBN 978-906419-77-6

First published in 2012 by Kevin Robertson
under the **NOODLE BOOKS** imprint
PO Box 279
Corhampton
SOUTHAMPTON
SO32 3ZX

www.noodlebooks.co.uk

Printed in England by Ian Allan Ltd.

Front cover: No. 31142 is heading south at Clay Cross Junction with an air conditioned Mk2 Open First and a Mk1 BG on 4th July 1985.

Preceding page: No. 47522 has emerged from Gasworks Tunnel into Kings Cross station with the empty stock of the 'Virgins and Clowns' Railtour on the morning of 21st April 1987. The first four coaches are a Mk1 BCK, two FO and a Mk1 Pullman, the tour departed behind 47418 and toured some of the freight only routes in the coal field areas of South Yorkshire and Nottinghamshire.

Rear cover: The 07:45 Kensington to St. Austell Motorail service passing Castle Cary behind No. 50018 'Resolution', 9th August 1980. The passenger accommodation is formed of eight Mark 1 coaches, all first class with the exception of the fifth vehicle, a buffet car, and the last, a brake first. Photo by Dave Payne.

Unless otherwise stated, all photographs are by the Author.

BR BLUE No 5

PASSENGER & PARCELS

John Dedman

Introduction

Welcome to volume No.5 in the BR Blue series of photo albums.

I have also been responsible for three previous volumes in this series (see inside rear cover):

BR Blue No.1 Southampton and The New Forest,
BR Blue No.2 Western Region, South and West,
BR Blue No.3 Freight in the 1980s.

All these generally covered the same period which is from the mid 1970s to the late 1980s. This latest book is intended to compliment No. 3 but now with the subject being Passenger and Parcels services.

Parcels trains are described in the working timetables of the period as 'N.P.C.C.S.' services, the abbreviation for 'Non Passenger Carrying Coaching Stock' but which also covers Mail and Newspaper trains. I have also included some trains with Departmental stock, but they are carrying staff rather than passengers.

Photos have been selected to cover a wide geographical area as much as possible. We start at Kings Cross and head north up the east coast to Scotland, then south to various areas in the Midlands, followed by a tour of the West Country and on to the South Coast finally terminating at Waterloo.

As referred to in the sub-title, the years covered are from 1975 to 1990. At the beginning of this period the blue livery was standard for locos, with blue and grey coaches and plain blue for most vans. Fifteen years later there was very little of the blue livery to be seen as new liveries were introduced during the 1980s. The change started in 1983 with a re-launch of the InterCity sector and with it the executive striped livery on High Speed Trains and the Mk2 Pullman coaches. In the following years this livery was adopted and applied to locos and coaches. Some variations and modifications occurred as time passed until it evolved as the well known InterCity 'swallow' livery which became the new standard. At the same time other sectors repainted their own allocated locos and stock to become known as Railfreight, Network SouthEast and Regional Railways.

For the period from the 1970s and into the 1980s there were a considerable number of different classes of loco in service, most types of which could be found on regular passenger and parcels trains. The exceptions are probably the dedicated classes of freight locos but even some of these would appear on summer holiday extras.

This book is intended to be use useful to the railway modeller with examples of train formations as well as carriage and van types from the period - especially the shorter trains that are shown.

For those perhaps slightly unaware of the various rolling stock codes applicable during the period, a basic explanation of these used in the captions is as follows:

Mk1	Mark 1 coach or van, built from 1951 to 1963
Mk2	Mark 2 coaches built from 1964 to 1975
Mk3	Mark 3 coaches built from 1975 to 1985
EMU	Electric Multiple Unit

DMU	Diesel Multiple Unit
BSK	Brake Second Corridor
BSO	Brake Second Open
BFK	Brake First Corridor
BCK	Brake Composite
BG	Brake Gangway – Full Brake
TSO	Second Open
CK	Corridor Composite
FK	First Corridor
FO	First Open
POS	Post Office sorting van
RMB	Miniature Buffet
RB	Restaurant Buffet
RK	Restaurant Kitchen
RKB	Kitchen Buffet
SK	Second Corridor
SLP	Sleeper Second
SLF	Sleeper First
TPO	Travelling Post Office
GUV	General Utility Van
CCT	Covered Carriage Truck

Of particular note is that in the 1970s there were still plenty of pre-nationalisation design bogie vehicles and BR four -wheel vans in use on parcels traffic. These included former GWR Siphons and Hawksworth full-brakes, LMS and LNER BGs, SR Utility vans and BR CCTs. Withdrawal of this older stock took place in the early 1980s, from which time parcel trains were composed of mainly BR BGs and GUVs, as will be seen in some of the later photos in this volume.

To supplement my own photographs, I have used some images from enthusiast friends, these are credited in the captions. The aim was to give the book a better geographical balance as well as a greater variation of train types. For these additional views I am very grateful to Dave Payne: for his 1970s Western Region photos, Peter and Keith Mantle: who seemed to have travelled the whole country during the 1980s, and John Fox and Pete Moody both who have kindly filled some gaps in my own collection.

Most of the views seen were taken on Kodachrome 64 and 200 slide film. Other film used included Ektachrome, Agfa CT18 and Fuji 100. A few were taken on Kodak Gold negative film. Cameras used were the Canon AE1 and AV1.

John Dedman.
Brockenhurst 2012

North from Kings Cross

Deltic No. 55002 'The King's Own Yorkshire Light Infantry' waiting to depart northwards from Kings Cross in September 1978. No. 55002 was repainted into its original two-tone green livery in 1980 and was finally withdrawn from service at the end of 1981. It is now part of the national collection at the York Railway Museum and is undergoing restoration by volunteers with the intention of restoring it back to running order.

On 20th April 1979 No. 31226 is seen at Finsbury park heading towards Kings Cross with a set of primarily air conditioned Mk 2d coaches. In addition there are two Mark 1s, the first a BG and the fourth a Buffet Restaurant catering vehicle. Both the latter having been fitted with replacement bogies to allow for faster running. This type of set formation /make-up was standard for many inter-city trains of the period.

EMU unit No. 312 710 is heading for Kings Cross at Brookmans Park on 9th October 1979. The class 312/0 25kV a.c. four car units were introduced in 1975 and used for Kings Cross outer suburban services.

Two class 105 two car DMU units make up the 2B53 09:38 Huntingdon - Kings Cross as it approaches Sandy on the 14th September 1977. These units were built to one of the earlier DMU designs, the first examples appearing in 1956.

Above: The 1S16 08:00 Kings Cross to Edinburgh has just passed Sandy on its high speed run north behind Deltic No. 55015 'Tulyar'. This was one of the Finsbury Park allocated Deltics which carried a racehorse name - perpetuating the similar contemporary names formerly worn on the Gresley 'A3s'. This engine escaped scrapping and is now being restored by the Deltic Preservation Society at Barrow Hill with the plan being to return it to the main line. The twelve coach train is made up of a BG, six TSO, an RKB, three FO and a BFK. 14th September 1977

Opposite top: No. 40057 piloting 47417 on the up Hull Pullman, in the book as the 1A02 06:50 Hull to Kings Cross, seen at Sandy on 14th September 1977. The first class accommodation is provided by the three Mk1 Pullman cars in reversed grey and blue livery whilst second class passengers travel in the air conditioned Mk2 coaches. Catering is supplied by a Mk1 RK and RMB in the centre of the train. This service called only at Doncaster and Retford on its journey to Kings Cross.

Opposite bottom: On the 14th September 1977 Deltic 55013 'The Black Watch' is approaching Sandy from the north with an express for Kings Cross. No. 55013 was allocated to Edinburgh Haymarket depot whose Deltic fleet was appropriately all named after Scottish regiments. The set of air conditioned Mk2 coaches are a BFK, two FO, two Mk1 catering coaches and three TSO.

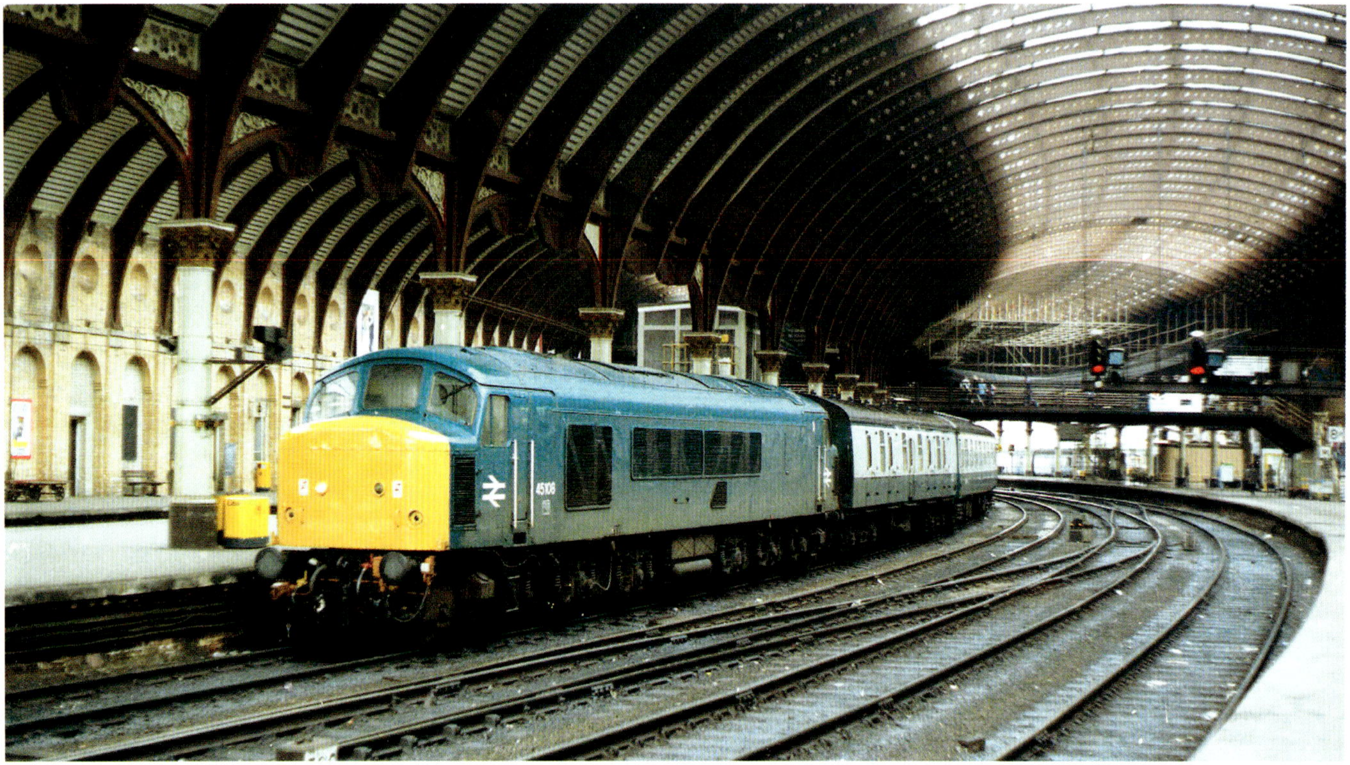
45106

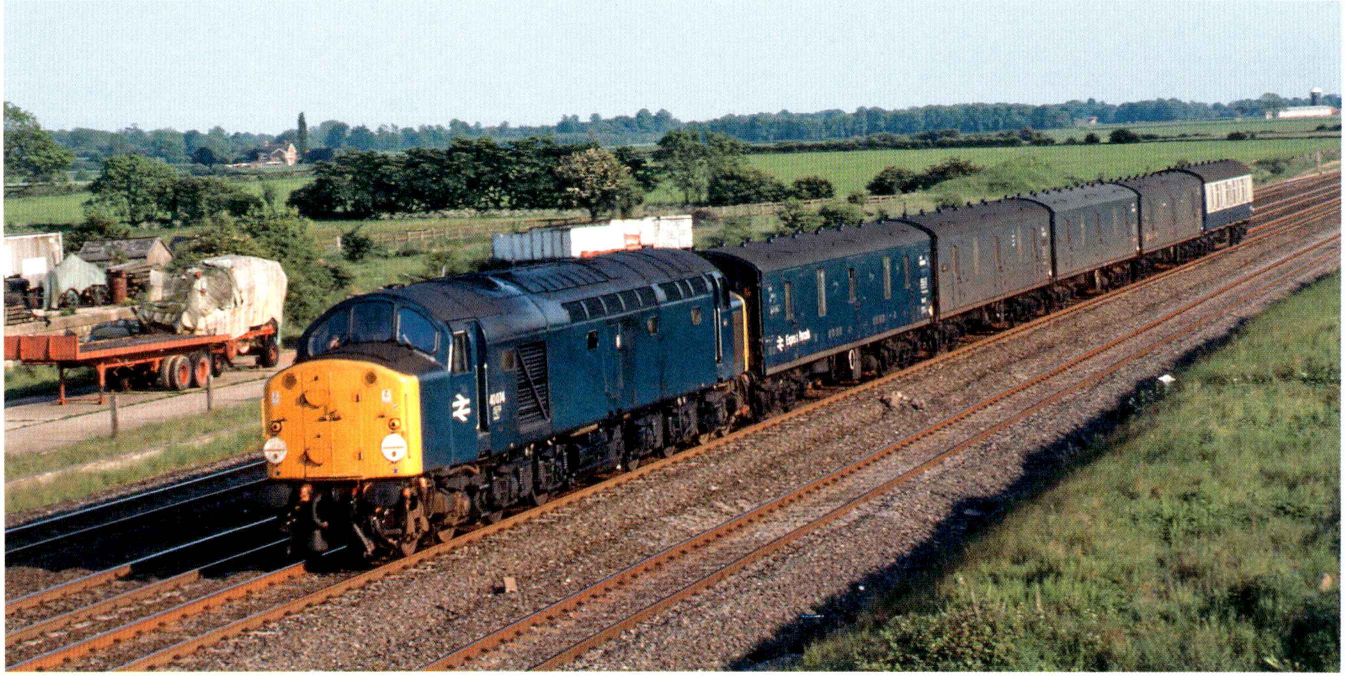

Opposite top: Peak class 45 No. 45108 stands under the unmistakable vista of the grand roof of York station in early 1985. The engine is at the head of a trans-pennine service linking the population centres of the east coast to those on the west coast. The class 45s were introduced from 1960 onwards. No. 45108 was originally numbered D120. Photo by Peter Mantle.

Opposite bottom: On 9th June 1980 40074 is heading north at the site of the former Otterington station on the East Coast main line. The train is a Parcels service consisting of four blue GUV vans and one blue/grey BG.

Above: The 17:56 York to Darlington is formed of a blue liveried two car class 101 DMU at Otterington on 9th June 1980. The leading vehicle is Driving Trailer Composite E56074.

Next page: As the sun sets the new era of a the High Speed train set on the East Coast main line is seen. The train at Birkby heading for Kings Cross., 8th June 1980. As introduced these units were numbered in the 254 series and consisted of eight passenger vehicles: five second class, a restaurant/buffet and two first class saloons. The Western Region HST sets, numbered in the 253 series, were similar except for being of seven coaches passenger cars having one less second class vehicle.

Into Scotland

No. 27005 is shunting empty coaching stock into the platform at Edinburgh in September 1985, it will then form a departure to Dundee. The Highland Rail stag logo is displayed on the side of the loco. Photo by Peter Mantle.

A two car dmu about to come off the southern end of the Fourth Bridge crossing the Firth of Forth at South Queensferry on 3rd June 1989. The bridge is one and a half miles long with construction completed in 1890.

Top: No. 47572 has charge of a Scotrail liveried push-pull set of Mk2 coaches as it heads south at Thornton North Junction on 26th June 1989. No. 47572 was named 'Ely Cathedral' at Ely in 1986 and still carries the Jack Sparrow logo of Stratford depot, despite being transferred to Bristol Bath Road depot the previous year.

Bottom: The 19:26 Dunblane to Edinburgh service near Linlithgow on 26th June 1989. Formed of three-car class 101 unit No. 356, the leading car is driving motor brake second No. 53253. The centre car appears to be a class 110 trailer second.

Waiting in the snow with empty coaching stock at Perth is 37043 'Loch Lomond'. The nameplates from this loco were later transferred to electric-heat fitted No. 37412 when it arrived in Scotland. No. 37043 then transferred south. 22nd February 1986. Photo by Keith Mantle.

The overnight 1S25 21:20 Euston to Inverness sleeper has almost reached the end of its journey as it approaches the summit at Slochd, 1,315 feet above sea level. Somewhat inappropriate perhaps is the locomotive, No. 47616 'Y Ddraig Goch/The Red Dragon' of Bristol Bath Road depot. 1ˢᵗ June 1989.

No. 37408 'Loch Rannoch' at Achanalt with the 12:27 Inverness to Kyle of Lochalsh on 29th June 1991. The Mk2z coaches, three TSO and a BSO are painted in LNER Tourist green and cream for use on this very scenic route.

Top: No. 37408 'Loch Rannoch' has just run round its coaches at Kyle of Lochalsh on 24th June 1991, the train being the 15:05 departure to Inverness. The first coach is an ex class 101 DMU Driving trailer converted to an observation car. The livery is LNER tourist green and cream and it carries the name 'Hebridean' on the green paint work. This conversion was used with a set of Mark 2z coaches in matching livery between Inverness and Kyle of Lochalsh.

Bottom: 37413 'Loch Eil Outward Bound' has the 20:25 Fort William to Euston Sleeper service near Spean Bridge on 22nd May 1989. Ben Nevis, Britain's highest mountain can be seen behind. Snow still lies on the high ground, highlighted by the approaching sunset.

North West England and the Midlands

Above: A class 503 EMU seen entering Birkenhead North with a service to Liverpool Central. At the head of this three-car unit is DMBS (Driving Motor Brake Second) No. M28372M. Electric supply is from a outside third-rail, similar to the SR system although powered at 650 volt d.c. system as opposed to 750 volts on the SR. Photo by Pete Moody.

Opposite top: Sandite spray vehicle No. ADB977047 stabled at Wigan Springs Branch depot on 22nd July 1984. This was originally a Driving Trailer in a Class 103 two car diesel multiple unit: its original number being M56156. The vehicle sprays Sandite, a gritty sand mixture on to the rails mainly in the autumn when leaf fall can cause loss of grip when both accelerating and braking.

Opposite bottom: Route learning car No. TDB 975023 about to enter Crewe station from the Manchester line on 13th October 1989. Prior to conversion for staff use, this was a single car class 122 No. W55001.

SANDITE
VEHICLE

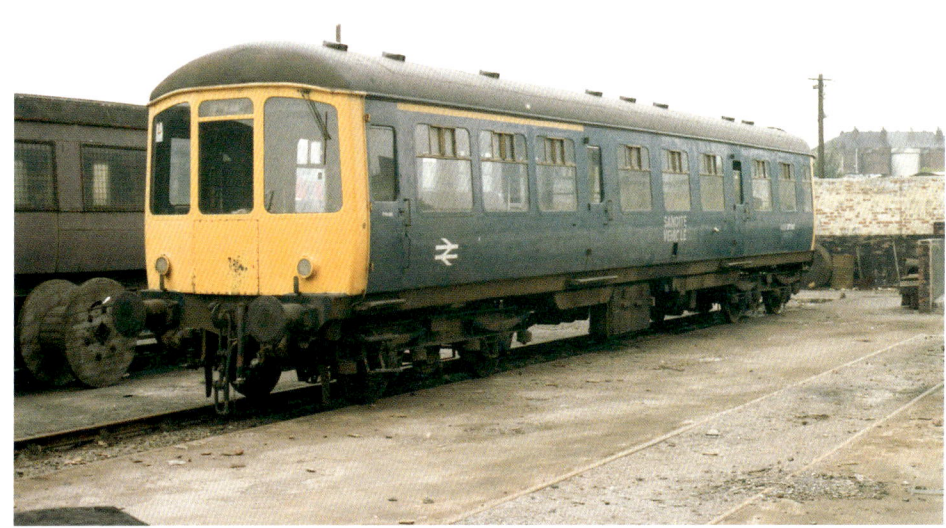

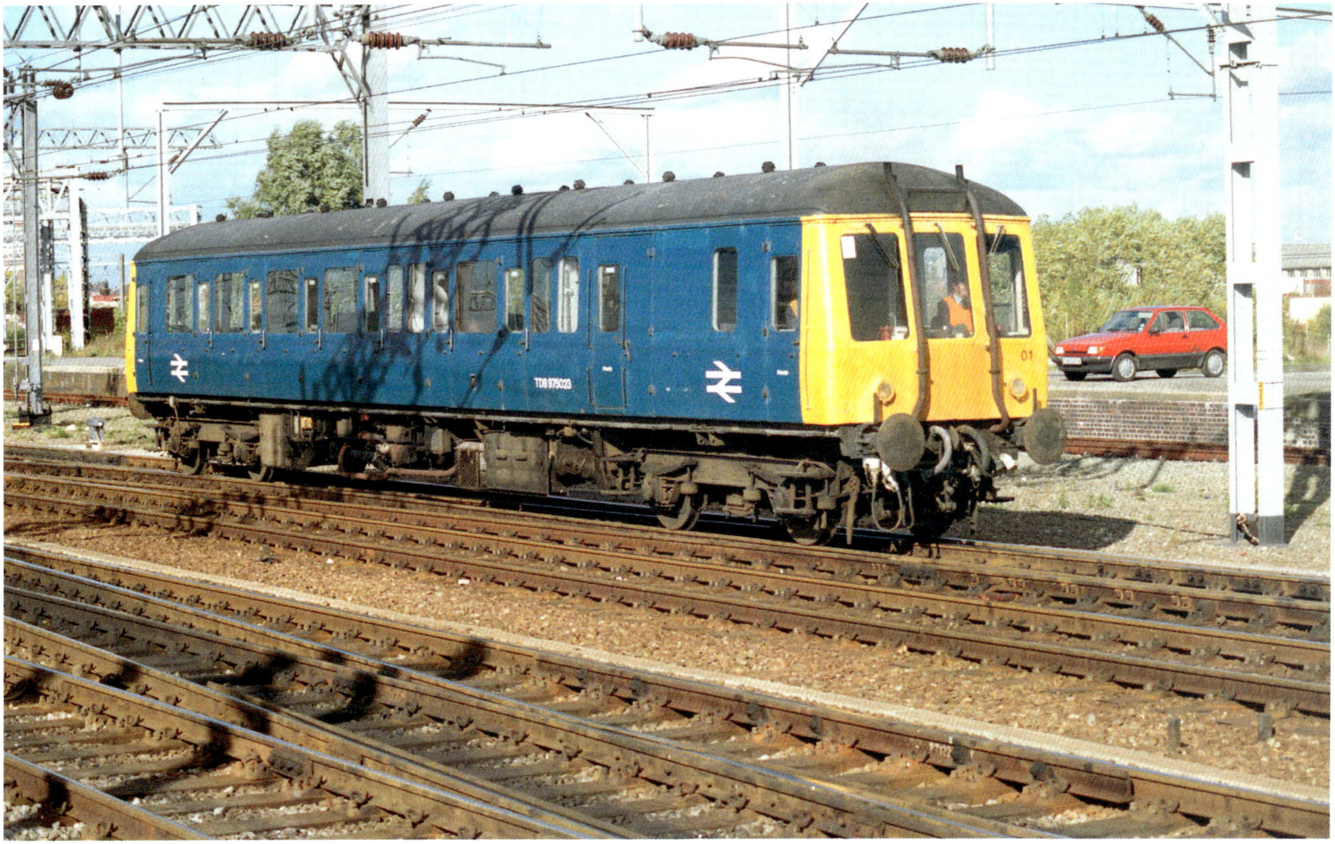
TDB 975023
01

Above: Class 304 unit number 006 arriving at Crewe with a service from Manchester Piccadilly. These units were built in 1960 as four car sets running on former Gresley bogies. Upgraded and refurbished in the mid 1980s they were reduced to three car units with the removal of the trailer composite. Photo by Pete Moody.

Left; A well worn looking No. 85028 departs north from Crewe on 13th October 1989 following a loco change. The train is the 1S64 09:08 Plymouth to Glasgow Central, the first vehicle identified as a Mk 2C Open Second.

Right: A short parcels train consisting of a BG and a GUV approaching Crewe on 13th October 1989. The loco is a one of ubiquitous class 47 type, No. 47456 in large logo blue livery. First put into service in 1964 as D1576 it was finally withdrawn in 1991.

Bottom: Class 87 AC electric No. 87026 approaching Stoke-on-Trent station with a train for London Euston, 22nd July 1984. No. 87026 is named 'Sir Richard Arkwright', an English inventor in associated with the 18th century cotton industry. The train is formed of a mixture of Mk 3, Mk2 and Mk1 stock.

Above: Speeding south towards Clay Cross Junction is No. 47319 with 1V98, the 16:02 Newcastle to Bristol parcels. The formation is four GUVs with a BG in the centre. Being overtaken on the up slow line is No. 56089 with a loaded MGR train, probably heading for Toton yard, Avenue sidings can just be seen in the background. 16th July 1986.

Left: No. 45118 has a load of five Mk1 coaches heading south towards Clay Cross Junction on 16th July 1986. The coaches are a corridor composite, a brake second, two seconds and another corridor composite at the rear.

The 10:15 Edinbugh to Harwich Parkestone Quay, known as the 'European', due to arrive at the Quay at 20:45 to connect with a Sealink ship to Hook of Holland. In charge is Stratford depot's No. 47584 'County of Suffolk', approaching Clay Cross Junction on 16th July 1986.

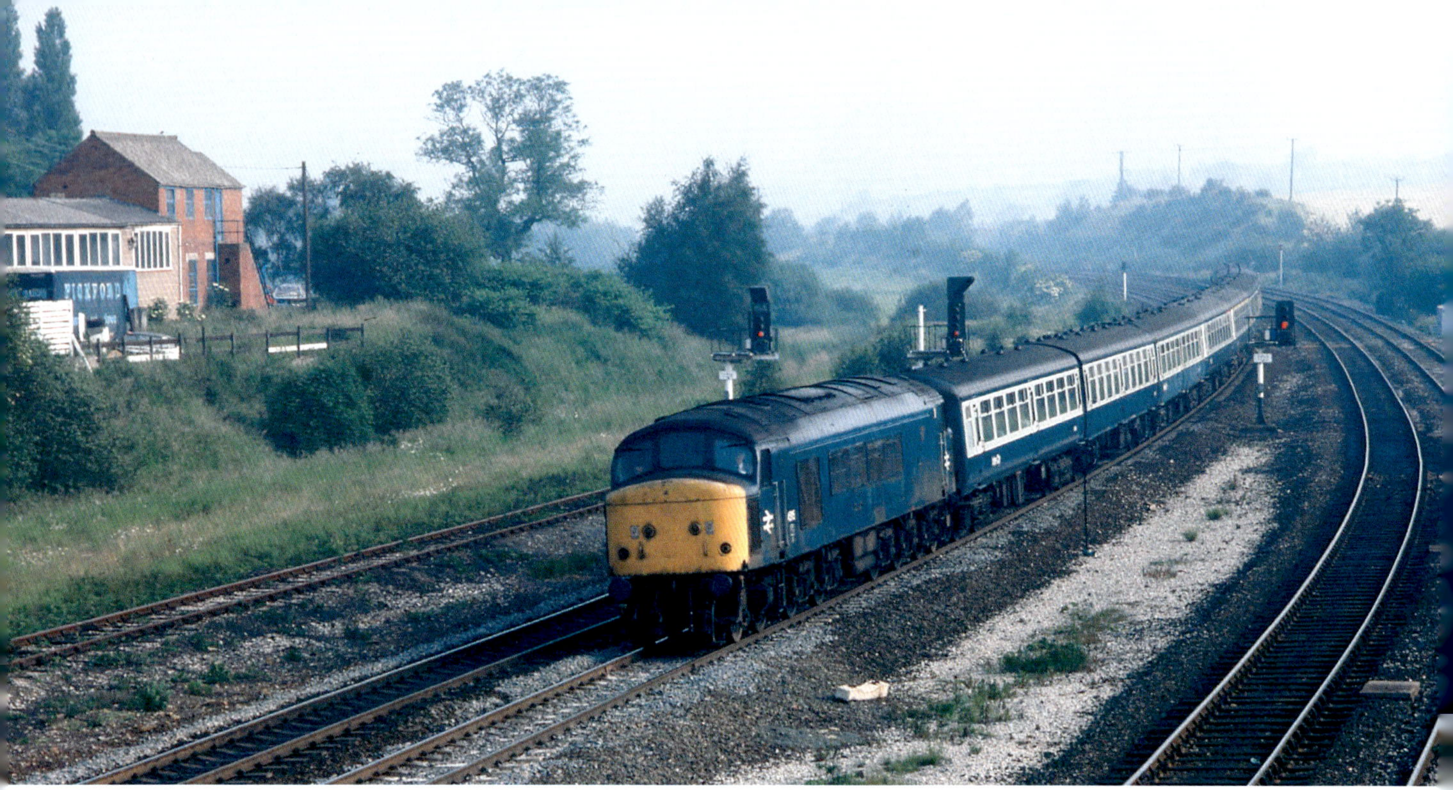
PICKFORD

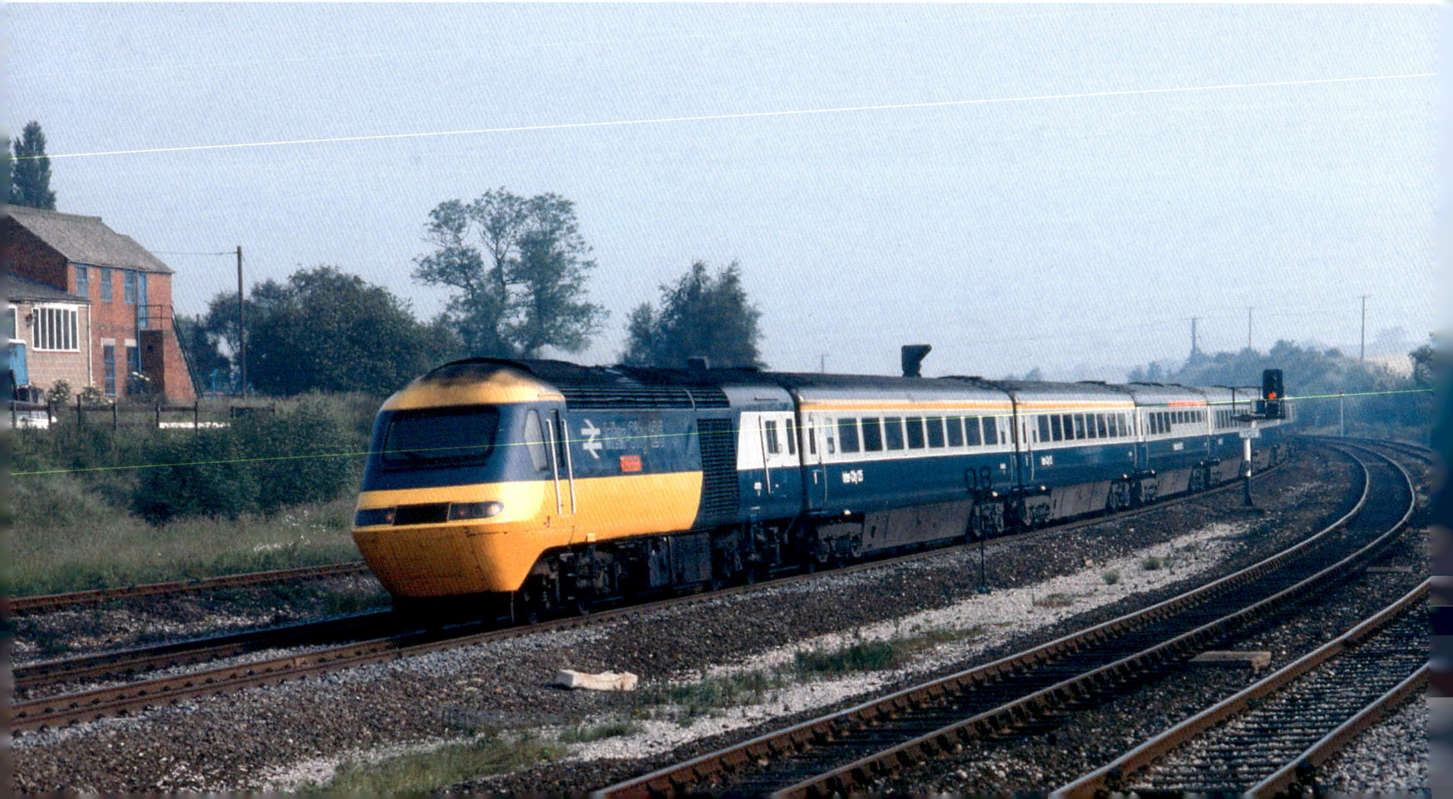

Opposite top: On 4th July 1985 No. 45115 is approaching Clay Cross Junction from the north with a mixed set of early Mk2 and Mk1 coaches.

Opposite bottom: A High Speed Train set forming the 07:12 Leeds to St Pancras seen approaching Clay Cross Junction on 4th July 1985. The front power car is No. 43152 carrying the name of 'St. Peters School York AD627' on a red plate. These distinctive plates were later replaced with a stainless steel versions following the introduction of the InterCity swallow livery.

Above: No. 47189 has come off the line from Derby at Clay Cross Junction with an APT test train. The train consists of two Railway Technical Centre coaches and four coaches from an APT set, including a power car. A driving trailer brings up the rear. The RTC coaches are RDB975422 'Prometheus' Laboratory 6, converted from Mk1 BSK No. 34875, followed by ADB975631 Test Service Car No.9, converted from FO No.3009. 4th July 1985.

Class 20 No. 20087 arriving at Toton yard from the north on 7th July 1987. In tow is QXV Inspection saloon No. DMDB 999504.

A very clean class 108 DMU has just passed Trowell Junction, Nottingham, with a local northbound service, 4th July 1985.

Left: Split headcode class 45 No. 45142 is departing Derby towards the south on 29th July 1978.

This page, bottom: No. 08842 shunting Mark 1 TPO vehicles at Derby station, 21st September 1988. The first TPO is a Stowage van which has doors on both sides, the second TPO a sorting van with doors on one side only (in this case the opposite side to the camera). Photo by John Fox

Opposite bottom: With a thunder storm about to break, a very short High Speed train heads south at Souldrop on the Midland main line, 26th August 1982. The formation consist of two power cars, a trailer guard second and two buffet cars, the rear power car seen to be from set No.254035. The combination was probably being used for driver training on this route as High Speed trains had yet to be introduced for services on the Midland main line.

Right: Double heading with class 45 locos did not seem to be very common especially with a light load such as this one of four vans. At 3.30pm on 7th September 1987 45150 and 45115 are heading south near Loughborough on the Midland main line. The stock consists of a GUV, BG, NNV and BG. The NNV is a Courier van which has been converted from a BSK, it has had some of its windows plated over and the installation of a set of roller shutter doors each side of the vehicle. The locos carry unofficial Tinsley Depot painted names, 'Vampire' and 'Apollo' respectively, 45150 has also been fitted with a high intensity headlight.

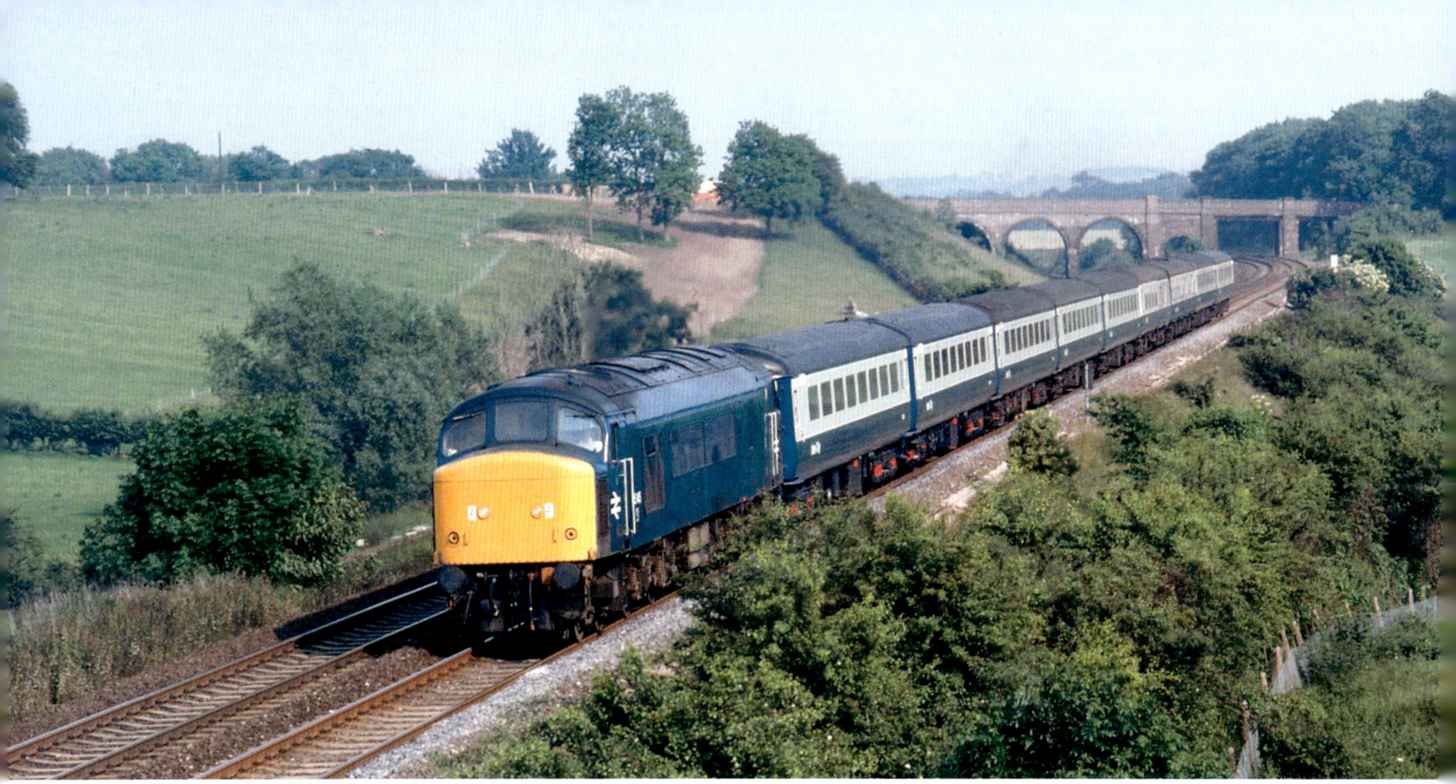

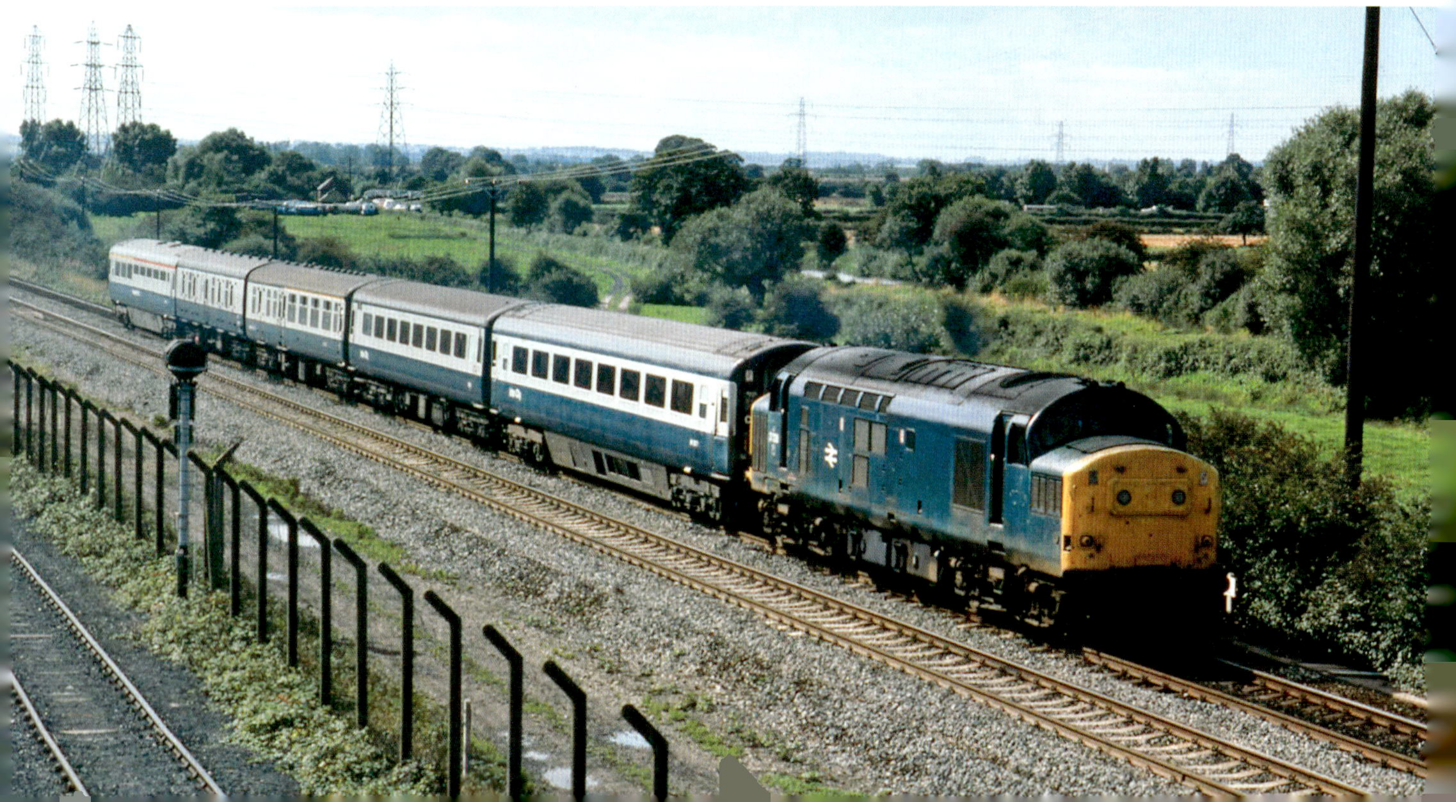

Opposite top: No. 45145 is heading north towards Sharnbrook summit on the fast line at Souldrop with the 16:30 St Pancras to Nottingham, 17th June 1982. The two slow lines are in a deep cutting out of site behind the train but the route can be seen where it passes under the arch of the bridge in the distance.

Opposite bottom: An empty stock train heading north at Willington on 7th September 1987 behind class 37 No. 37226. The stock is a varied mix of Mk1 , Mk2 and Mk3 coaches.

Above: Southbound near Portway, a ten car formation of DMU vehicles in blue/grey livery, 19th June 1986.

Above: The 1V64 12:47 Newcastle - Plymouth Parcels is near Portway north of Tamworth on 19th June 1986. It is formed of No. 45051 and six blue GUVs.

Opposite top: Heading north on the West Coast main line south of Rugby is No. 86230 'The Duke of Wellington'. Unusually there are two Mark 3 Sleeping cars marshalled at the front of the Mark 2 coaches. 11th June 1986.

Opposite bottom: No. 87008 'City of Liverpool' is caught at speed with a southbound train at Bletchley on 27th June 1980.

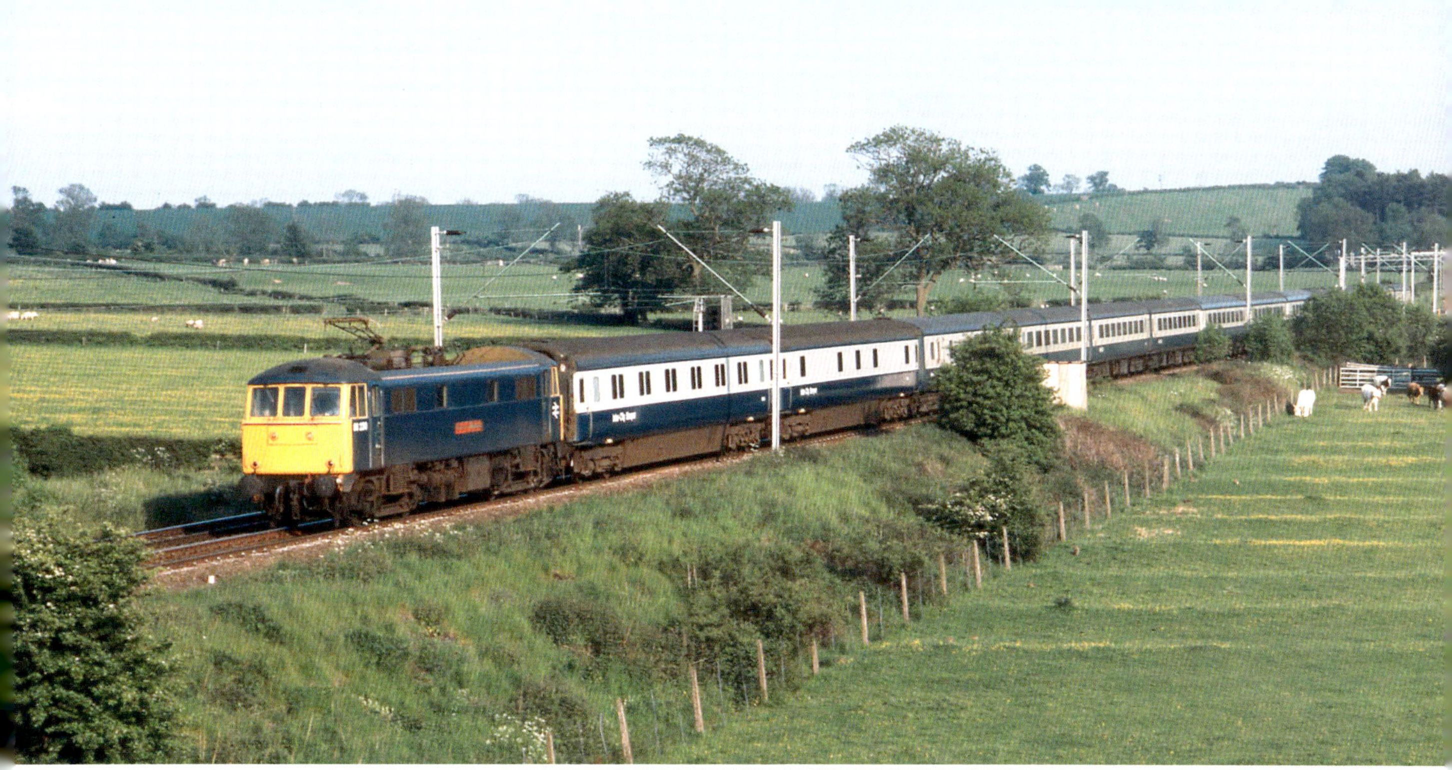

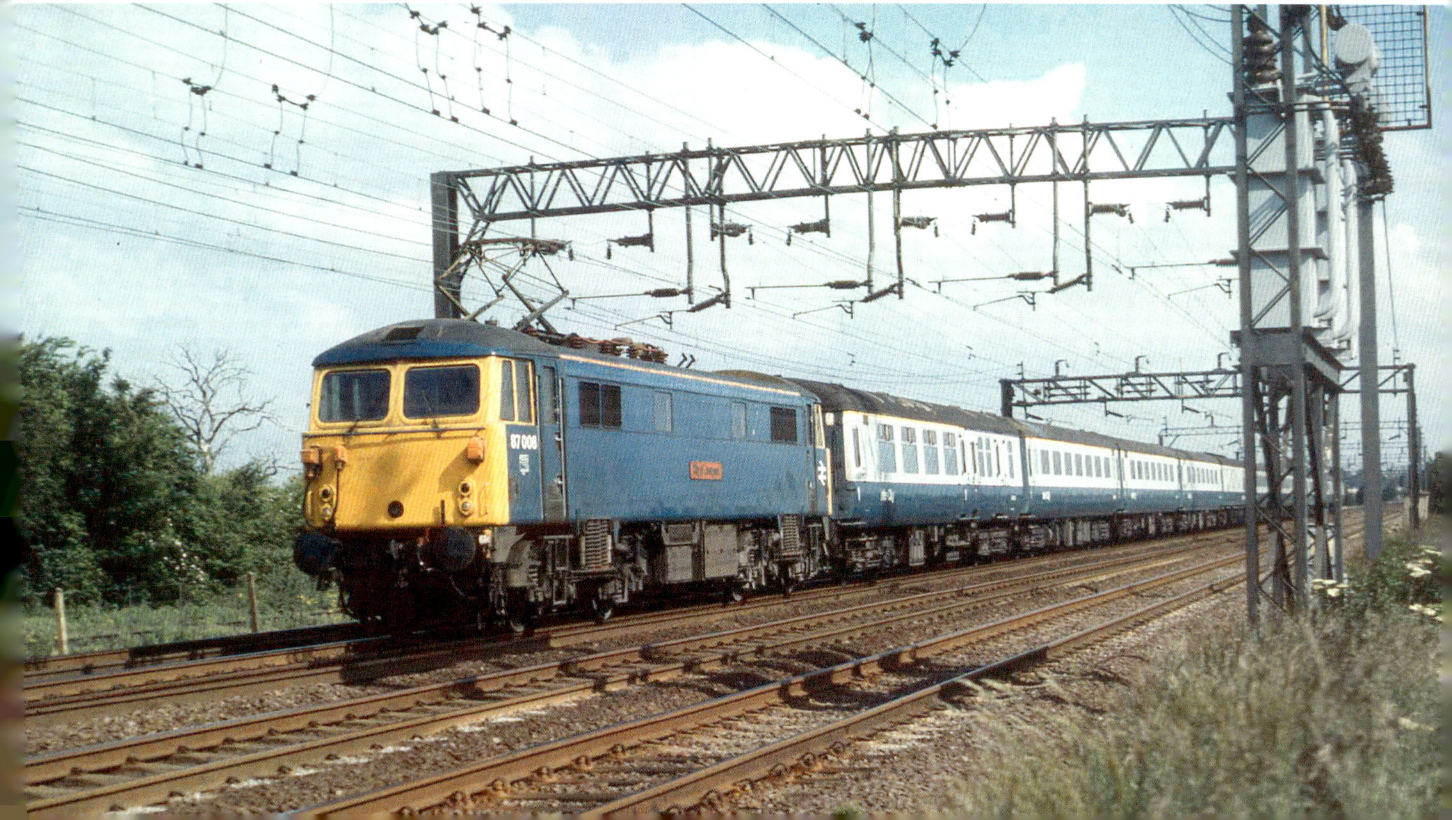
87 008

Above: An unusual formation seen heading north on the slow line at Bletchley, 27th June 1980. No. 86011 has a Railway Technical Centre coach and a BG in tow. The RTC coach is ex-East Coast main line Mk1 Pullman Car, No. 323 now in the RTC livery of blue and red. In its new guise it is Laboratory coach 14 and carries No. RDB975427 and the name 'Wren'. It was used by the RTC from 1974, mainly for testing interior noise levels until withdrawn in 1988 and then sent for scrap.

Opposite top: In the winter sunshine class 85 No.85022 is heads south at Bletchley with a short parcels service. The train is made up of two BR GUV vans both with Express Parcels labelling. 26th January 1980.

Opposite bottom: The down morning 'Manchester Pullman' which had left Euston at 08:00, is caught at speed near Bletchley on 27th June 1980. The loco is No. 86230 'The Duke of Wellington'. One of the two Parlour Kitchen cars has been replaced by a Mk1 RKB Buffet Kitchen coach which can easily be picked out by its standard blue and grey livery amongst the reversed livery of the Pullman cars.

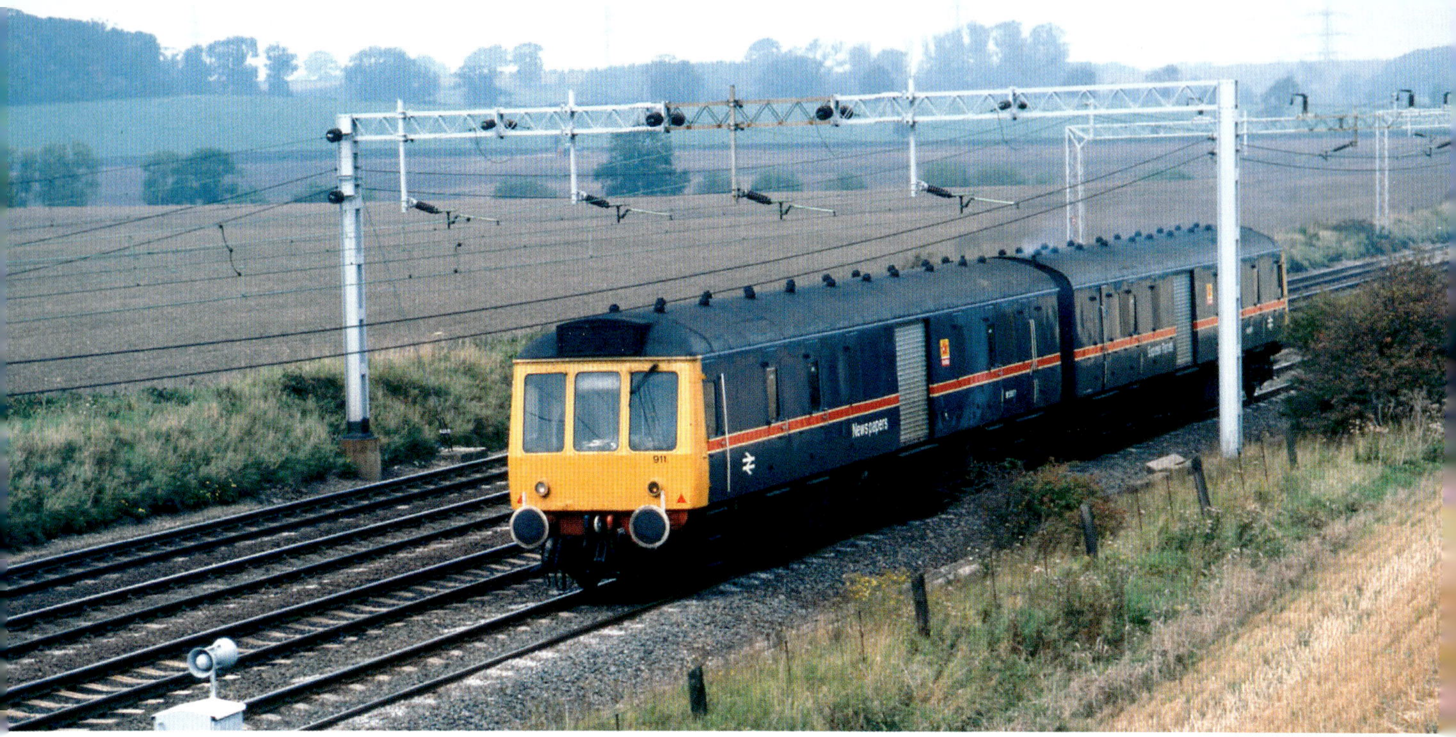
911
Newspapers

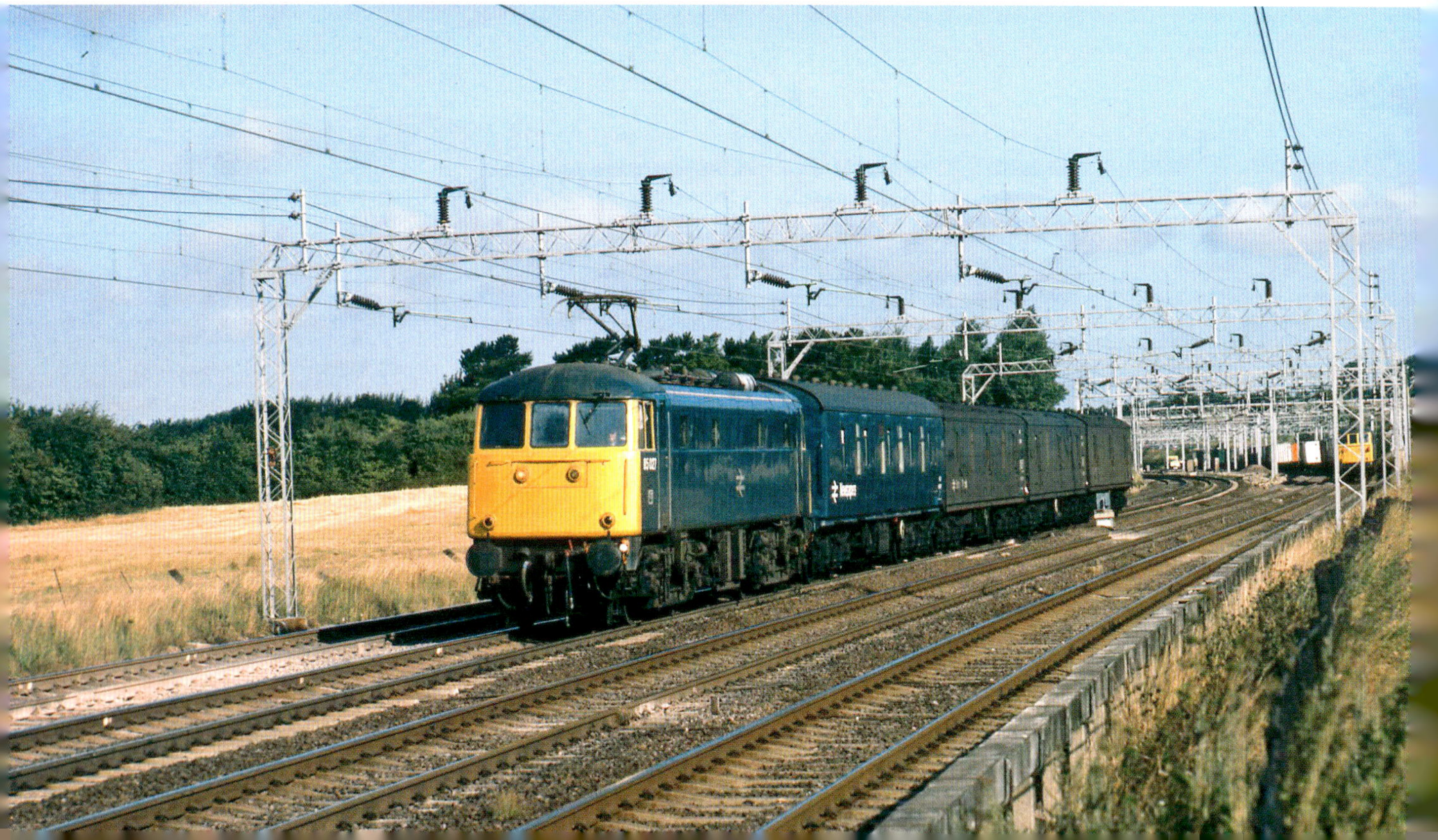

Opposite top: Two-car Red Star parcels liveried unit number No. 911 travelling south on the West Coast main line near Linslade, 30th September 1986. This unit is formed of two former class 127 power cars Nos. 55971 and 55981 which have been converted for parcels and newspaper use, including the installation of roller shutter doors.

Opposite bottom: A short van train consisting of a BG and three GUVs hauled by No. 85027 heading south at Tring on 26th August 1982. All the vans are in plain blue livery with the BG labelled 'Newspapers'

Above: An overnight service from the north heading south at Tring with No. 86246 at the head on 26th August 1982. The first coach is a TPO sorting coach - the red letterbox can be seen on the side. The rest are Mk1 coaches with a BG, a sleeper second and a sleeper first before the day coaches. Coming into the picture from the left is No. 85034 hauling an oil train the detail of which was shown in BR Blue No.3.

Left: A west coast main line overnight train has just passed Tring in the early morning on 26th August 1982. It is headed by No. 86242 'James Kennedy GC' hauling ten Mark 1 sleeping cars with a BG at the rear. The sleeping cars alternate between second and first class through the formation, as can be identified by the yellow cantrail band on the first class cars.

This page, top: No. 86248 is heading north on the down fast line at Tring with Mk2 air conditioned stock on 17th June 1982, at the same time overtaking class 310 unit No. 086 on the down slow line.

This page, bottom: No. 81019 on the down slow line at Tring with an empty stock train of just a single Mk1 coach, 26th August 1982. The vehicle is No. M9225, a brake second open - code BSO. This coach type has more seating and a smaller luggage area than the much more numerous brake second corridor, code BSK. Note the tail lamp is positioned on the lower tail lamp bracket, a higher bracket is positioned to the left side of the corridor connection. This differential was deliberate so that if two coaches both carrying tail lamps were joined together, the lamps would not collide.

Class 501 electric multiple units lined up at Watford Junction just after sunrise on 30th January 1985. Nearest the camera is No. 501 186. These unit were used to operate the local service to Euston picking up their current from the 630v dc third rail. The same type of set was used for services from Broad Street to parts of North London.

Celebrity loco No. 86235 'Novelty' at Watford Junction on 7th April 1983 with the 07:56 Euston to Manchester Piccadilly 'Manchester Pullman'. This was one of two intermediate stops for this train, the other being Wilmslow. The engine was named 'Novelty' during the commemorative 150th anniversary of the Railnhill trails of the original Liverpoool and Manchester Railway.

Class 86/0 No. 86033 heads south at Bushey with a Parcels working made up of Mk1 BG and GUV vans, 7th April 1983. This loco has been fitted for multiple working hence the jumper cable and receptacle to the front end. It was later fitted with SAB resilient wheels and Flexicoil suspension and reclassified as class 86/4 No. 86433.

Right: No. 25050 has a light load of one Mk1 BG as it passes through Bushey station travelling on the up slow line towards Willesden. 7th April 1983.

Bottom: Heading towards Euston at South Kenton is No. 86220 'Goliath' with a short parcels train of a single BG and two GUVs. 7th April 1983.

West from Paddington

Opposite top: No. 81012 arriving at journeys end -Euston station - October 1985. The coaches are a mixture of Mk1 and Mk2 stock whilst on the side of the loco is the salmon symbol of Glasgow depot. Photo by Peter Mantle.

Opposite bottom: With the loco crew chatting in the comfort of their cab, No. 87031 is being coupled to its Inter City liveried coaches at Euston, 21st April 1987. No. 87031 bears the plate 'Hal o' the Wynd', a name previously carried by a 4-4-0 steam loco No. 62417 withdrawn in 1951.

Above: At 12:44 on 10th April 1981, No. 31118 exemplifies the comments made in the introduction over the longevity of some former pre-nationalisation stock. Seen is an up van train passing through Sonning Cutting with in order behind the loco a BR GUV, a Southern 4-wheel van, another GUV, five Great Western Siphon's: two of which have been recently repainted, two BR Mark 1 BGs and at the end two more GUVs. Photo by Dave Payne.

Class 128 Motor Parcels Van No. W55991 heads into Sonning Cutting on its journey from Paddington to Reading, 12:30pm, 10th April 1981. These single car units were introduced in 1959, with this one and sister No. W55992 (see below) were employed on parcels services between Paddington and Reading. Photo by Dave Payne.

An interesting combination of single railcars bound for Reading on the down slow line in Sonning cutting, 16th August 1985. Nearest the camera is blue liveried No. W55992, coupled to a class 121 unit in blue/grey livery. Photo by Dave Payne.

No. 47433 near the east end of Sonning cutting on 10th April 1981 with the 10:45 Weston-super-Mare to Paddington service. The coaches are a set of Mark 3 vehicles from a High Speed train, the power cars removed and substituted by a Mk1 BG at either end.

Caught at speed as it leaves Sonning cutting is No. 50024 'Vanguard' in charge of the 09:50 Paignton to Paddington. The train is made up of a typical rake of air-conditioned Mark 2 coaches of the period with a Mk1 BG behind the loco and a Mk1 Restaurant/ Buffet car separating the first and second class accommodation. 1st May 1981. Photo by Dave Payne.

Left: Oxford station on 27th April 1980 witnesses No. 08656 shunting vans of different railway ancestry. The first is an ex LMS BG followed by two SR PMV, a BR GUV, another SR PMV and a final BR GUV. Photo by Pete Moody

This page, bottom: With the City of Bath as a backdrop class 119 DMU unit No. B578 enters the station in October 1973. On the left is a class 31 still carrying its pre-tops number of (D)5826, and with in original green livery save for full yellow ends. Photo by Dave Payne.

Opposite page, top: A scene which can never be repeated at Severn Tunnel Junction on 7th May 1986. No.47117 passes with an up parcels working comprising two GUV vans and a Mk1 BG. At the then stabling point in the background can be seen locos of classes 37, 45, 47 and 56.

Bottom: The skyline of Newport is in the background as No. 33065 heads towards Cardiff with four withdrawn Mk1 coaches. Most have had their windows broken and are probably on their way to one of the South Wales scrap yards. 7th May 1986.

Above: Class 101 unit No. C804 is at Swansea on 4th September 1986. This two-car set is made up of Driving Motor Brake Second No. 51452 and Driving Motor Composite No. 51523. The first-class accommodation is at the far end, indicated as usual by the yellow cantrail stripe. Photo by John Fox.

Opposite top: A class 119 2 Car unit approaching the Ferryside station stop on 3rd July 1987 as the 16:34 Milford Haven to Swansea. The unit is No. C577 and consists of a Driving Motor Second and a Driving Motor Brake Composite.

Opposite bottom: Following the bank of the East Looe River is Class 121 single car unit No. W55026 forming the 14:57 Looe to Liskeard service, Monday 2nd July 1979. At the time there was a seven train a day shuttle in each direction between the junction at Liskeard and the terminus at Looe. Thirty plus years later the branch is busier still with twelve return trips a day by 2011. Photo by Dave Payne.

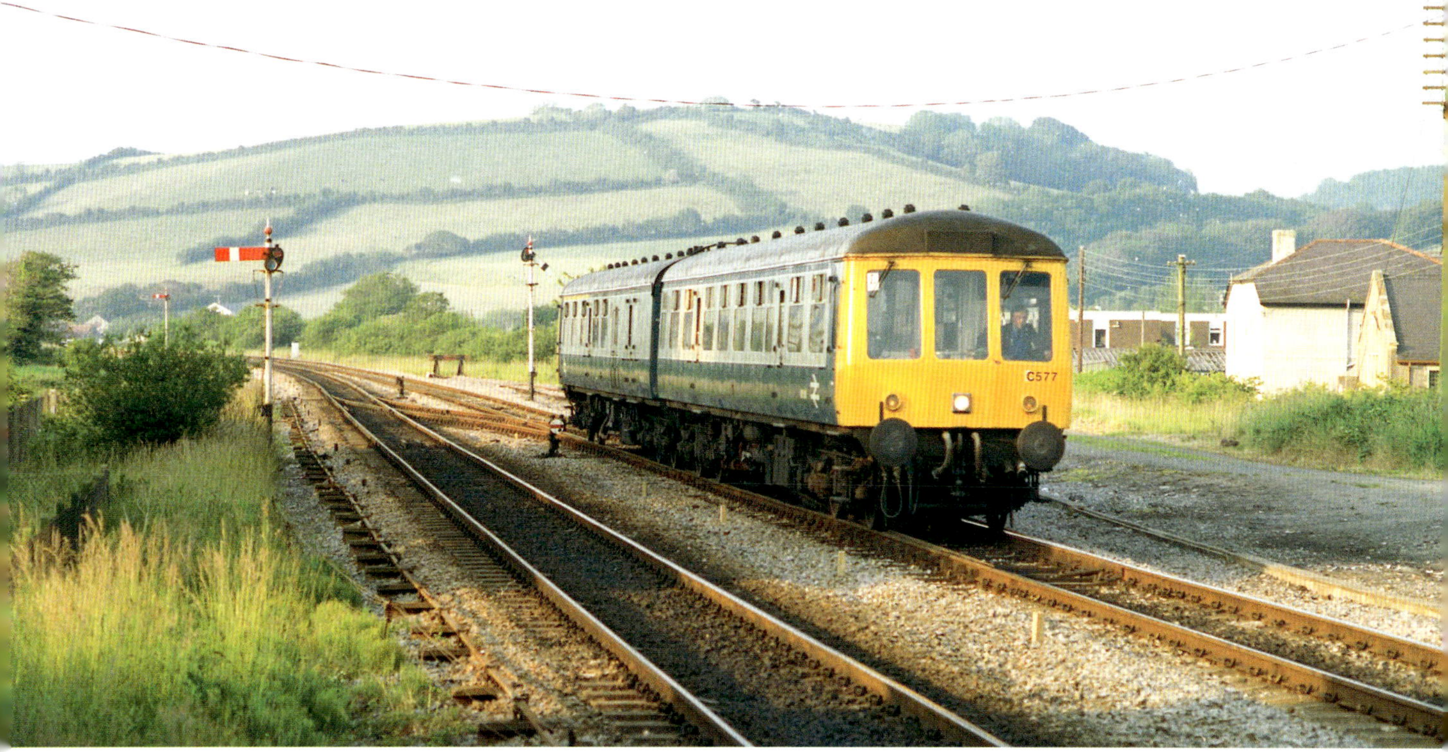
C577

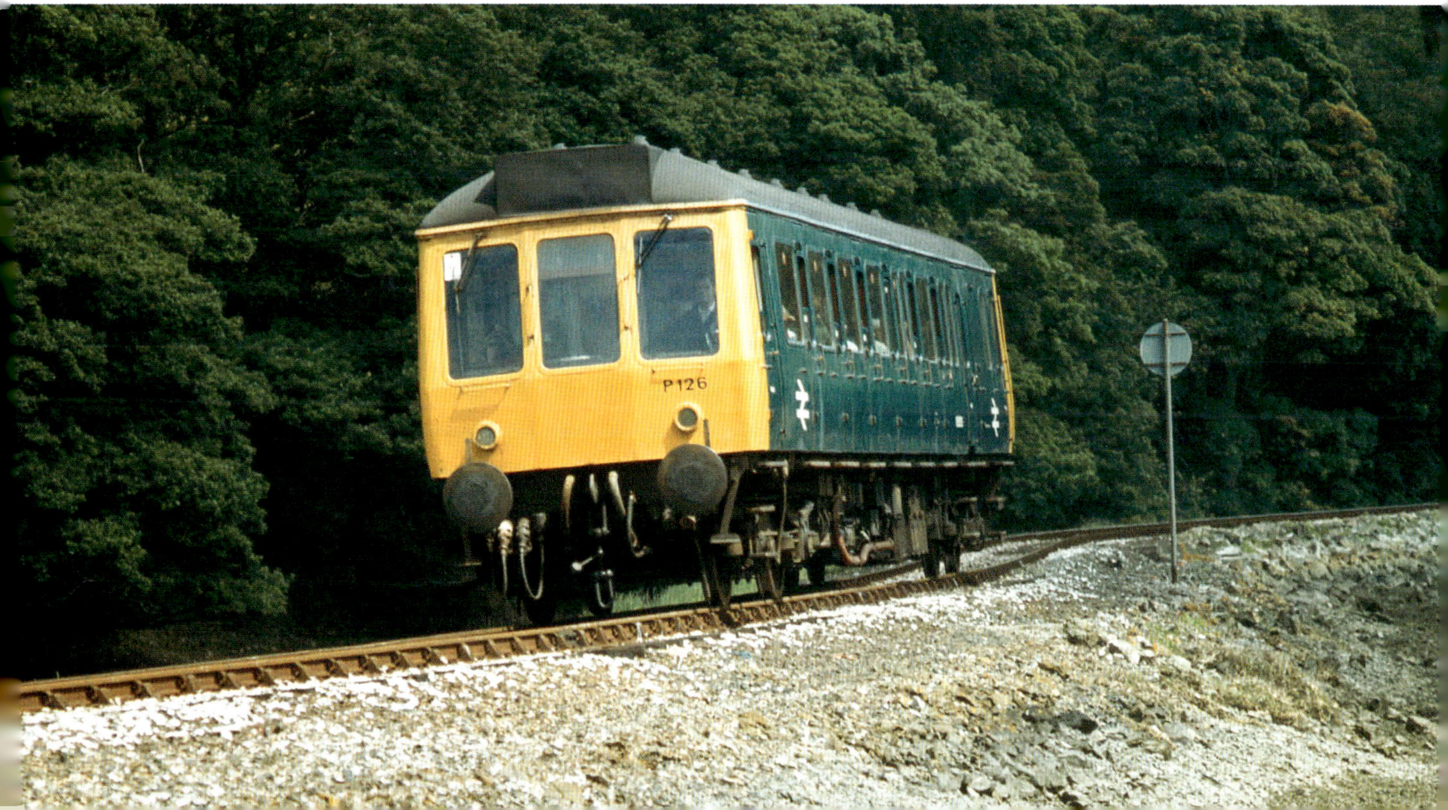
P126

Above: Liskeard station is the location as the 12:03 Penzance to Paddington High Speed train approaches for its stop at 13:31, Saturday 18th April 1981. The leading power car is No. 253 001 with No. 253 015 bringing up the rear. The siding on the right contains a set of OCV china clay hood wagons. Subsequent rationalisation of resources has witnessed the removal of these sidings. Photo by Dave Payne.

Opposite top: An unidentified class 46 has just crossed from Cornwall into Devon over the famous Tamar bridge. The train is the 07:40 Penzance to Leeds service comprising of Mark 1 coaches on the 18th August 1976. Photo by Dave Payne.

Opposite bottom: On the 5th July 1979 46014 powers up Hemerdon bank with a set of Mk1 coaches forming the 09:02 Penzance to Manchester service. Photo by Dave Payne.

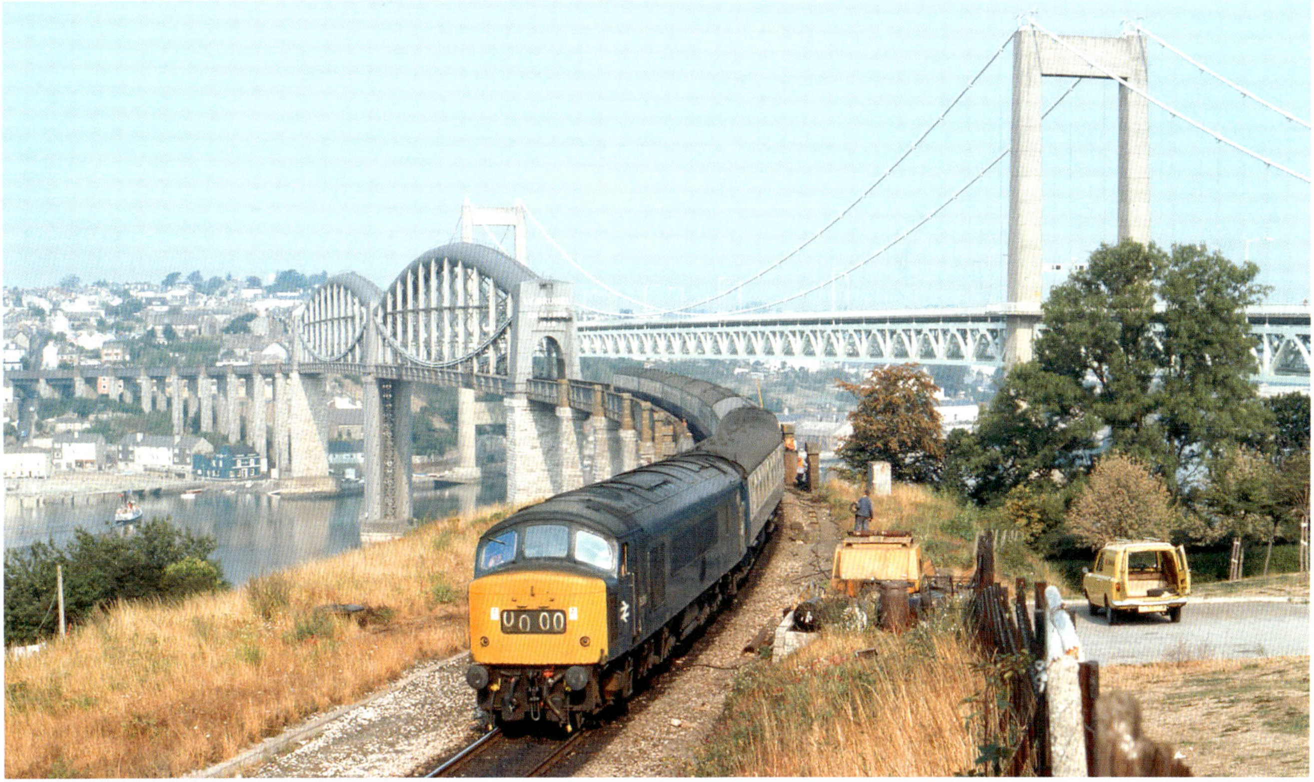

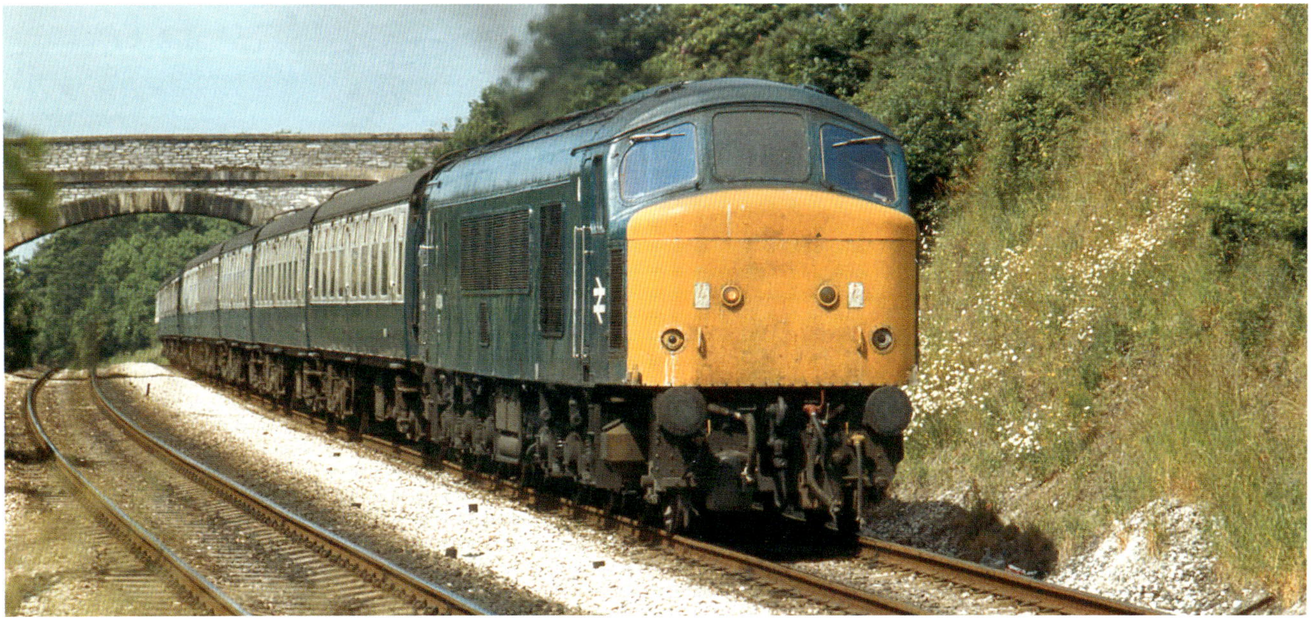

Above: No. 50025 'Invincible' seen approaching Newton Abbott from the east at 11:23 on 11th August 1978. The train is the 07:45 Kensington to St. Austell Motorail service: the car carrying vehicles being out of site at the rear of the train. Passenger accommodation was solely first-class, the coaches all 1st class corridors with the exception of the fourth which is a RU Buffet car and the eighth which is a Mark 2 brake first. Photo by Dave Payne

Opposite top: Large logo class 47 No. 47552 passing Dawlish on the south Devon coast, 24th June 1989. This loco is still in service today as part of the DRS fleet, but now carrying the number 47802 and name 'Pride of Cumbria'. Photo by Keith Mantle.

Opposite bottom: Seen in strong evening sun at Dawlish Warren on 16th May 1986, unit B450 a class 117 with a class 101 trailer composite as the centre car, forms 2C49, the 17.48 Paignton to Exmouth.

The 16:10 Barnstaple to Plymouth dmu is about to traverse the level crossing at Exeter St Davids station on 11th August 1978. The train is formed of a three car class 118 set No. P470 with a GUV attached as tail traffic to the rear. Photo by Dave Payne.

Above: An attractive scene at Cowley Bridge Junction where the former Southern route from Barnstable joins the WR main line to Exeter. On 13th June 1981 class 31/4 No. 31423 is coming off what was once a main line but now very much a branch and crossing the River Exe with the 12:08 Barnstaple to Exeter service. The coaches are a Mk1 SK, Mk 2 TSO, Mk 1 CK and Mk 1 BSK. Photo by Dave Payne.

Right: On 13th June 1981 No. 50004 'St Vincent' is at Cowley Bridge Junction with the 10:05 Penzance to Paddington Cornish Riviera'. The loco is hauling a failed High Speed train, the rear power car No. 253 031. Photo by Dave Payne.

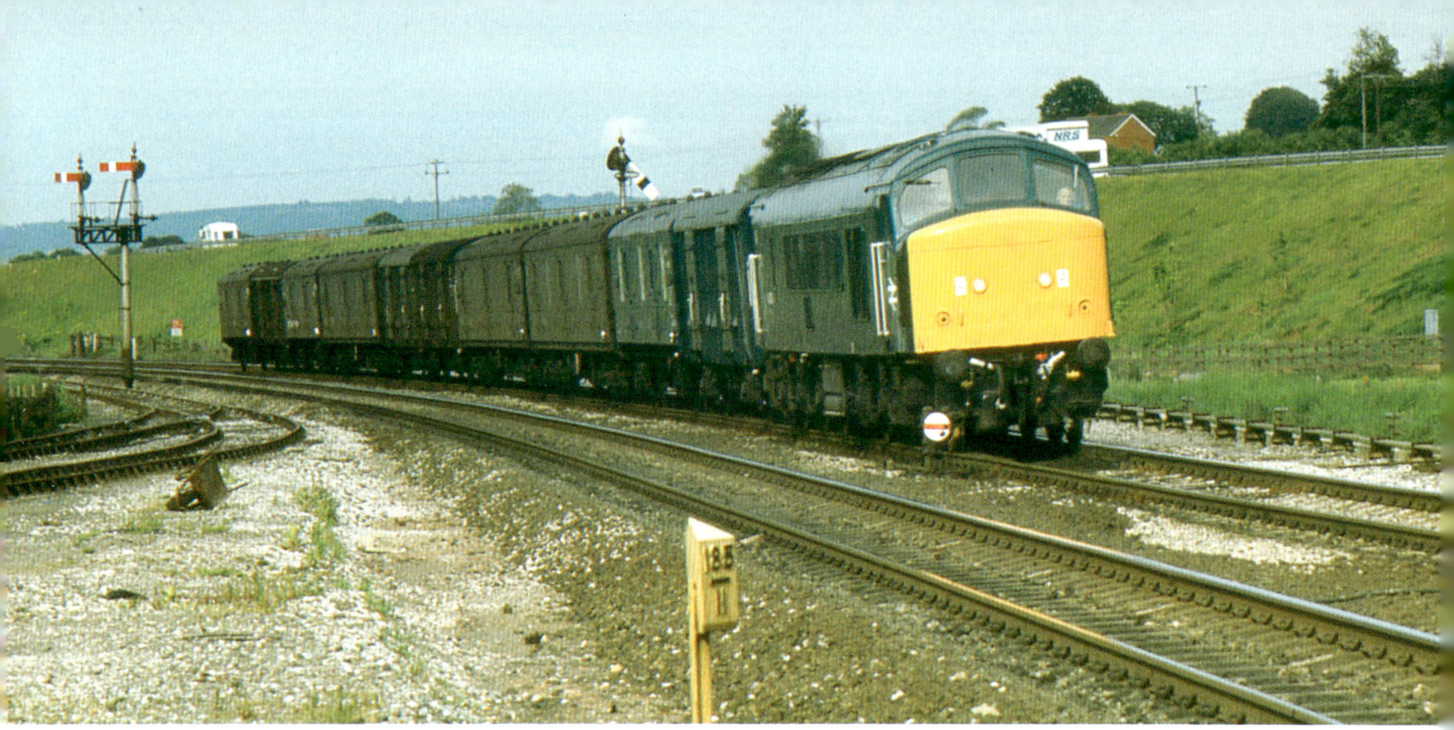

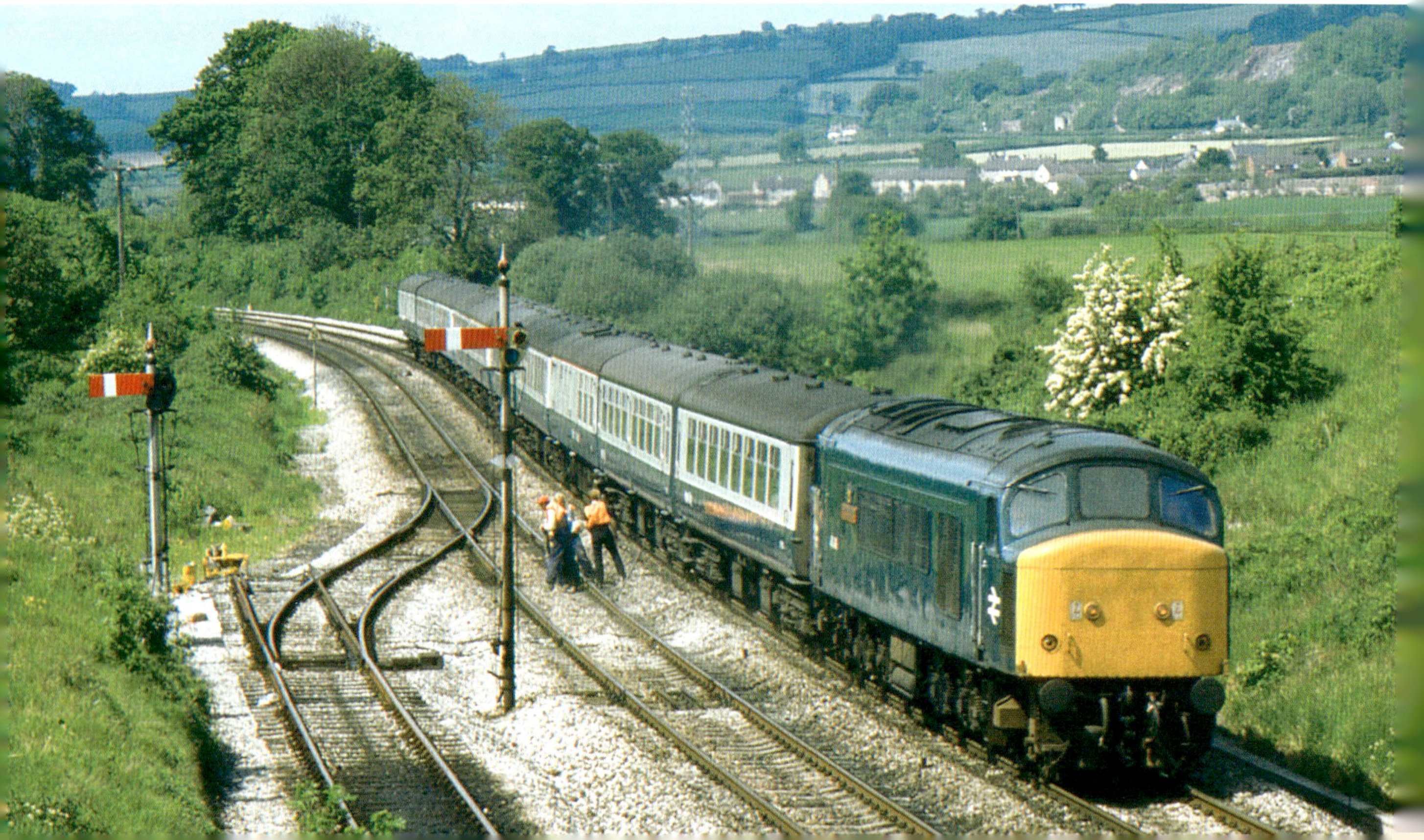

Opposite top: Class 46 No. 46008 heads an early evening parcels train west towards Exeter near Hele and Bradninch, 30th May 1980. The vans are a mixture of ex-SR CCT Utility vehicles , BR CCTs and BR GUVs. At the top of the embankment is the M5 motorway, road and rail running parallel with each other for about seven miles as far as the former Tiverton Junction. Photo by Dave Payne.

Opposite bottom: No 45049 'The Staffordshire Regiment, (The Prince of Wales's)' is nearing the summit at Whiteball from the direction of Exeter, 30th May 1980. The train is the northbound 07:40 Penzance to Liverpool service. Photo by Dave Payne.

Above: No. 47439 is west of Whiteball tunnel on 17th June 1978 with the daytime 12:35 St. Austell to Crewe Motorail service. This has the usual Motorail compliment of first class corridor coaches where each car booked had a compartment allocated for its occupants. The overnight services, which mostly ran to Scotland, also included sleeping cars. Photo by Dave Payne.

With all six power cars smoking well, the 08:42 Cardiff to Weymouth service accelerates away from Castle Cary on to the branch destined for Yeovil, Maiden Newton, Dorchester and Weymouth. Again once an important main line, the remaining single track indicates the route's now branch-line status. In the background is the former GWR 'ARP' wartime signal-box, a possibly unique example in view of its white paintwork. The nine car formation is led by class 117 unit No. B427 in August 1984. Photo by Dave Payne.

Above: With an assortment of BG and GUV vans in tow, No. 31317 comes off the new 'cut-off' and is passing the signal box at Clink Road Junction, 10th August 1979. The now singled track to the right is the original route to Frome which will rejoin the later cut-off a few miles further west at Blatchbridge Junction. The original Frome line also has a junction to the ARC stone quarry at Whatley. Photo by Dave Payne.

Above: An unidentified class 52 Western diesel is passing Great Cheverell with a Paddington bound service from the West Country in October 1973. Photo by Dave Payne.

Opposite bottom: The 16:14 Bristol to Weymouth arrives at the Westbury complex from the north. The importance of this location both as a junction and stone hub is exemplified by the lines of (temporarily) empty stone wagons probably awaiting available space at the nearby quarries. The loco is No. 31423 with three Mark 1 coaches: a corridor second, a corridor composite and a brake second open. 9th August 1980. Photo by Dave Payne.

Southern Region lines

Drawing the gaze from a number of spectators, No. 33117 crawling along Weymouth Quay with the Channel Island Boat Train, 6th August 1983. The front of the loco has been fitted with an orange flashing light and a bell for its journey through the streets. Here it has just passed under the Town Bridge, a section of line prone to regular flooding at very high tides.

The Boat Train seen now on its return journey from the Ferry Terminal. The regular loco-hauled boat train ran until the end of the 1985 summer season and was replaced the following year with TC stock, linking the Quay with Weymouth Town station.

Above: No. 37428 heading up the gradient from Upwey towards Bincombe with the 2V91 18:15 Weymouth to Cardiff Central on 1st July 1990. The four Mk2 Network SouthEast coaches are a Corridor Brake First and three Open Seconds. Three years earlier on 16th May 1987 at Pwllheli, this loco had been named after the WW1 Prime Minster 'David Lloyd George'. Photo by Keith Mantle.

Opposite top: On 2nd June 1988 the signal box at Branksome is under repair as 47659 passes with the empty coaching stock of the 1O03 22:00
Edinburgh to Poole sleeper. After terminating at Poole the coaches are taken to Bournemouth West depot for servicing and stabling before returning to Poole for the evening departure. No. 47659 was later renumbered 47814 and became a Virgin Trains loco. It was subsequently rebuilt as class 57 No. 57306 still with Virgin. Photo by Keith Mantle.

Opposite bottom: Early morning sun illuminates the lofty position of the signal box above Bournemouth station on 13th May 1988. Miniature snow plough fitted 33015 is waiting to leave with the 2B20 07:25 departure to Eastleigh. This is an all stations stopping train with vans and coaches. This stock was the return working of the 1Y01 02:45 passenger and newspapers vans from Waterloo - also the final day of this working. Photo by Keith Mantle.

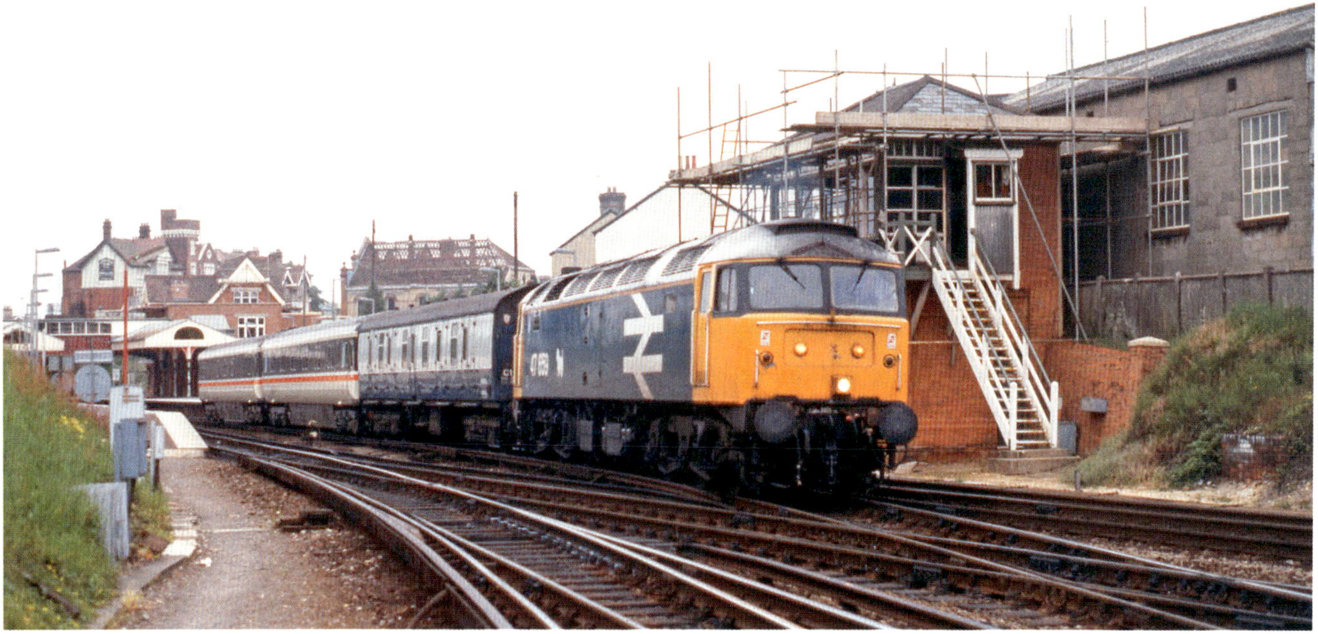

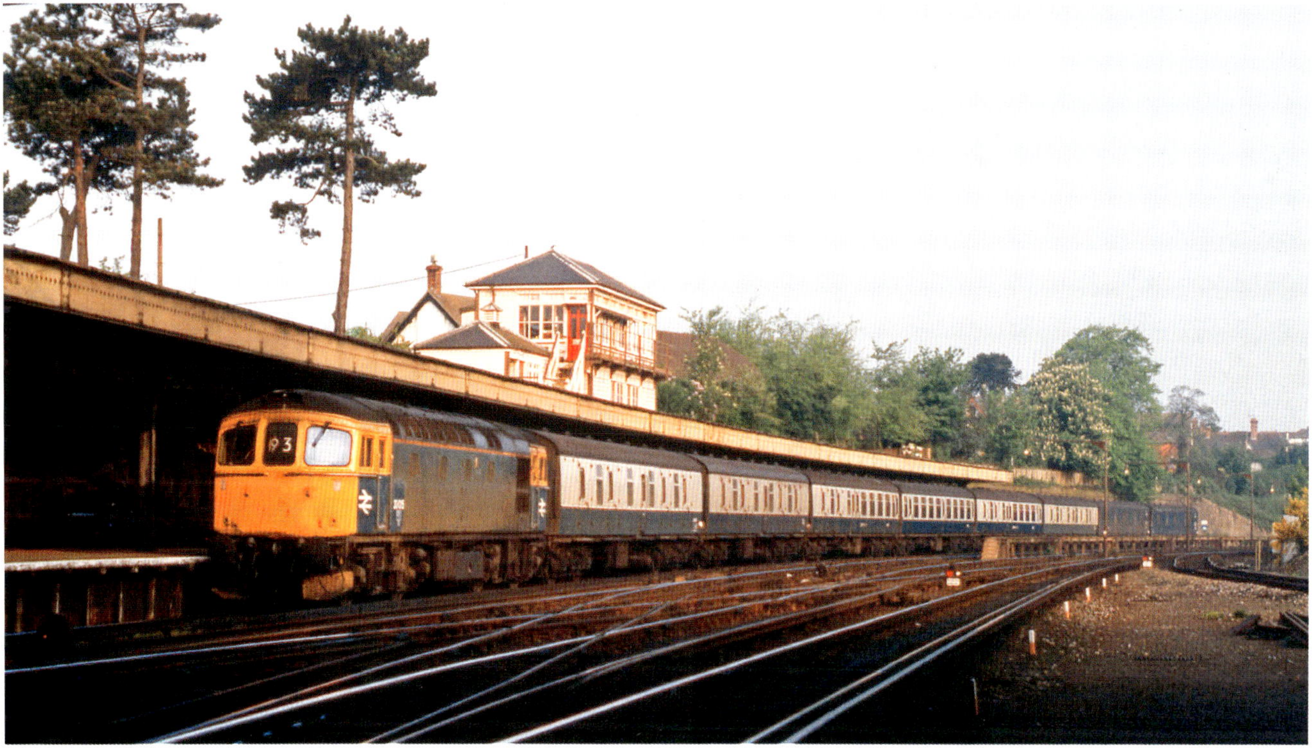
93

No. 47664 is working hard as it tackles Christchurch bank with an inter-regional Poole to the north of England service, 2nd February 1989. The mixed colour formation were typical of the late eighties on these services, indicative of the cross over from the corporate to the sector liveries. Photo by Keith Mantle.

A Waterloo to Bournemouth, headcode 92 (semi-fast), service formed of a twelve car, 4TC+4TC+4REP, combination. The train is approaching Beaulieu Road station in the New Forest, 29th May 1984. Although having a slightly longer journey time between Waterloo and Bournemouth compared with the fast (headcode 91) service, the 'semis' were far more taxing to work considering the stops made and the need to accelerate hard to maintain the schedule.

On 19th March 1983 the 'Thames Piddle Executive' railtour visited the Fawley branch on the west side of Southampton water. It is seen here heading south near Marchwood. The special was comprised of two Hastings Six-Car class 202 units No. 1032 leading No. 1017.

A 3H Unit, known locally as a 'Hampshire' about to stop at Millbrook station with a headcode 77 Portsmouth to Salisbury stopping service. The set, No. 205 026, displays its new sector ownership with Network South East flashes on the cab front and coach side. 18th May 1989.

Electro-diesel 73139 in Southampton (Western) Docks shunting a Mk1 BG at the Post Office Mail/Parcels depot in 1985. The BG had been tripped from Southampton Central station where it had been detached from the rear of the InterCity train from Manchester. Photo by Keith Mantle.

Class 73 Electro-diesel 73136 approaching Southampton Central with the Sunday only 4B46 12:10 Bournemouth to Clapham Yard Parcels. The vans are a Mark 1 BG, LMS BG and three GUVs.
19th February 1984.

Left: Passing under Horseshoe Bridge at St Denys is the 3B04, 09:45 Southampton to Clapham empty vans, 16th June 1988. The loco is No. 33027 'Earl Mountbatten of Burma' hauling five GUVs, an exhibition coach and an Express Parcels BG

Opposite bottom: As can be seen from its exhaust the class 08 on depot duties is working hard shunting GUVs and coaches at Eastleigh on 4th June 1987. The photo is taken from the Campbell Road bridge which gives access to the depot and works and has always been a popular viewpoint for railway enthusiasts. Southampton Airport can be seen on the horizon, the South Western main line leading to Southampton and Bournemouth to the right.

Above: A comparison of diesel and electric multiple unit ends at Eastleigh Depot on 14th April. From left to right are class 204 3T No. 204003, class 414 2Hap No. 6051 and class 421/2 4Cig No. 7343. Photo by John Fox.

No. 56047 heads west past East Grimstead quarry with three withdrawn class 405 4-SUB electric units, 18th May 1984. A number of these sets had congregated at Eastleigh after withdrawal and following removal of usable material were stored opposite the station. A few found a temporary lease of life being loco hauled by EDs, the intention being to give drivers experience when working locomotives with an EMU combination. Such times were short lived and the SUBs were eventually despatched to the breakers. Here unit No. 4742 can be seen bringing up the rear.

The inside of Eastleigh Depot is the location for Class 205 3H unit 205025 on 14th April 1987. As seen before, the new ownership is displayed with the addition of Network SouthEast logos to the erstwhile BR blue/grey livery. Photo by John Fox.

In its first Summer of service the Victoria Simplon Orient Express is seen east of Ashford behind 73142 'Broadlands'. The re-furbished Pullman coaches are owned by Sea Containers Ltd and form the first leg of the journey from Victoria to Folkestone Harbour, the passengers will then board a ferry to France to connect with the Continental train to Venice. 19th August 1982.

A pair of class 73s in large logo blue livery await departure with trains of BG and GUV vans at Waterloo station, 28th April 1987. On the left is No. 73104 and on the right with a Bournemouth line headcode No. 73003. Photo by John Fox.